THE BRITISH LIBRARY

Souvenir Guide

CONTENTS

LEFT: *Entrance to the British Library from the Piazza. Photograph by John Donat*

FRONT COVER: *(foreground) The entrance gates to the British Library, designed by the Cardozo Kindersley Workshop, from a photograph by Irene Rhoden*
(background) Detail from the Sforza Hours, a book of hours produced in Italy and the Netherlands, c.1490 and 1517, illuminated by Giovan Pietro Birago and Gerard Horenbout. British Library Add. MS 34294, f.233v.

PAGE 1: *Detail from the Bedford Hours (see page 22), the story of David and Bathsheba. British Library Add.MS 18850, f.96*

BACK COVER: *The Gutenberg Bible (see page 31)*

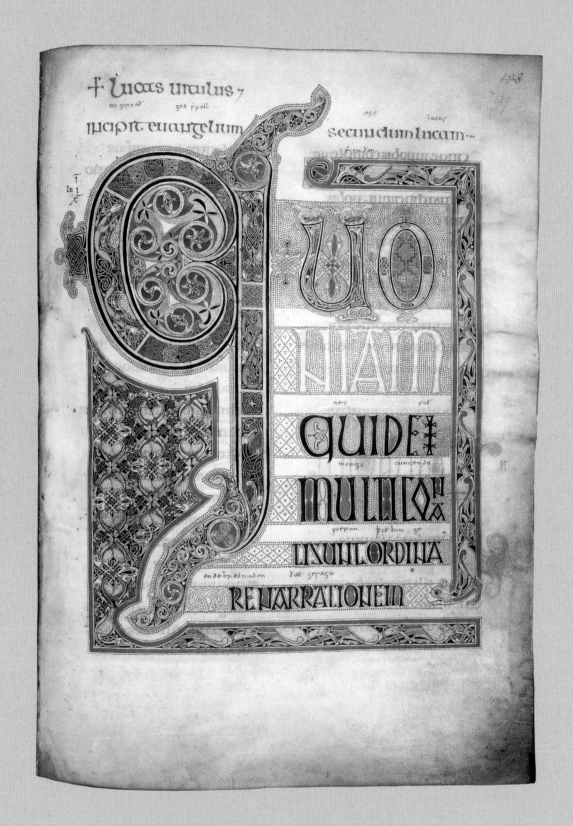

✝ Lucas uvailus 7

incipit euangelium   secundum lucam ∴

QUONIAM QUIDEM MULTICON LISUNCORDINA RENARRATIONEM

FOREWORD

The British Library's splendid new building at St Pancras opened its first reading rooms in autumn 1997, providing a fine new working environment for scholars and researchers. As well as serving the needs of readers, the new Library offers an innovative and varied exhibition programme, and on 21 April 1998 we welcomed the first visitors to our three new, purpose-built exhibition galleries – the John Ritblat Gallery: Treasures of the British Library, housing many of the most highly prized items from the Library's collection; the Pearson Gallery of Living Words, with a range of changing themes; and the Workshop of Words, Sound and Images, an interactive environment inviting visitors to learn about aspects of communication.

Many of the Library's finest treasures in the John Ritblat gallery are featured in this souvenir guide. Their range and scope are unparalleled and give some flavour of the richness of the Library's collection. Many of them are part of the magnificent heritage of books, manuscripts, maps, and music which together formed the 'foundation collections' of the British Museum in 1756, and which passed to the British Library when it was established in 1973. Others are the result of generous donations or acquisitions since.

We warmly and gratefully acknowledge John Ritblat's support and that of the Pearson Group who have made these galleries possible, and look forward to welcoming visitors to them from all over the world, to enjoy and share our delight in the treasures they contain.

John Ashworth
Chairman

OPPOSITE: *The Lindisfarne Gospels, major initial page at the opening of the Gospel of St Luke. Lindisfarne, c.AD 698. British Library Cotton MS Nero D iv, f.139*

INTRODUCTION

The British Library – Britain's national library – was established in 1973, as the result of an Act of Parliament which brought together a number of bodies into a single organisation, principally the library departments of the British Museum, the National Central Library, the British National Bibliography, the National Lending Library for Science and Technology, and the Office for Scientific and Technical Information. The new national library operated on several sites, including the British Museum in London, and Boston Spa, near Wetherby in Yorkshire. In 1975 the Government acquired a site by St Pancras station to house a new building which would bring together the majority of the Library's London-based collection in a single home, offering enhanced access for the public and improved conditions for preservation and storage. The first Reading Rooms of the new British Library building, designed by Professor Sir Colin St John Wilson, opened in 1997.

The British Library holds one of the world's great collections of books and manuscripts. Its treasures span almost three millennia and come from all the continents of the world. They include some of the most famous of all documents: the Lindisfarne Gospels, a supreme example of the illuminator's art; the Diamond Sutra, the world's earliest printed book; Gutenberg's 42-line Bible, the first western book printed with moveable type; and Shakespeare's First Folio. Other items such as Magna Carta have their own crucial place in history, while among the many thousands of literary manuscripts are copies of some of the best-known works of English literature, from 'Beowulf' to 'Alice's Adventures Under Ground'. In addition there are rich collections of other materials – maps, music, stamps and sound recordings – all of which include world-renowned works.

Although the Library's own history is relatively short, many of its collections were originally brought together nearly 250 years ago upon the foundation of the British Museum. The British Museum Act of 1753 established a museum to hold the collections amassed by the antiquary and collector Sir Hans Sloane (1660–1753), Sir Robert Cotton (1571–1631) and Robert (1661–1724) and Edward Harley (1689–1741), first and second Earls of Oxford. Forty-one Trustees were charged with control of the new institution, to preserve the collections 'for Public Use, to all Posterity'. The library of the Museum became the first public library in Britain, providing access to its collections in a reading room serving 'all studious and curious Persons'.

OPPOSITE: *Sir Eduardo Paolozzi's statue of Newton, after Blake, seen through the entrance gates.*
Photograph by Irene Rhoden

Sir Hans Sloane, a physician, antiquary, and President of the Royal Society, had left his large collection of books, manuscripts, prints, drawings, coins, medals, antiquities and natural history specimens to trustees, with instructions to offer it to the nation for £20,000. Parliament agreed to the purchase, and authorised the organisation of a lottery to finance a new museum. The collection of Sir Robert Cotton, which had been vested in trustees for the use of the public in 1700, was also handed over to the British Museum by the 1753 Act. His unparalleled manuscript collection included the Lindisfarne Gospels and two of the four

The entrance hall, with the tapestry woven by the Master Weavers
of the Edinburgh Tapestry Company, after R.B. Kitaj's painting 'If not, not'.
Photograph by John Donat

surviving original texts of Magna Carta. At the same time as acquiring the Sloane and Cotton collections, the Trustees of the Museum purchased, for £10,000, the library of Robert Harley, first Earl of Oxford and his son Edward, the second Earl.

These three 'foundation' collections were accommodated in Montagu House in Bloomsbury, and by 1759, when the new Museum opened to the public, they had been further enlarged by the receipt of the Royal Library, a gift from George II. Dating from the 1470s, this collection had been added to by successive monarchs, and contained thousands of manuscripts and printed books. This royal gift established the tradition of presenting and bequeathing private libraries to the British Museum Library, and many other notable

The rear of the King's Library tower
which houses the collection of King George III, given to the nation by George IV.
Photograph by John Donat

figures followed suit, including the actor David Garrick, the naturalist Sir Joseph Banks, and the book-collectors C.M.Cracherode and Thomas Grenville. When King George IV donated his father George III's collection known as the King's Library in 1823, Montagu House was too small to accommodate the newly acquired collection of over 60,000 volumes, so between 1823 and 1827 a special gallery was built to hold it. This was the beginning of the construction of the present British Museum building designed by Sir Robert Smirke.

The great development of the British Museum Library took place in the middle of the nineteenth century as a result of the efforts of Antonio Panizzi (1797–1879), a political refugee from Italy, who was Keeper of Printed Books from 1837 to 1856 and Principal Librarian of the Museum from 1856 to 1866. Panizzi supervised the compilation of a new catalogue of printed books and vigorously enforced compliance with the 1842 Copyright Act, which required the deposit of a copy of every British publication in the Museum Library. Between 1837 and 1866 the Keeper of Manuscripts, Sir Frederick Madden (1801–1873), also made considerable additions to the collection of western manuscripts.

Soon after the completion of Smirke's new Museum building in 1852, shortage of space for the library led Panizzi to plan a new Round Reading Room, surrounded by four cast-iron book stacks, in the central courtyard of the Museum. The impressive new domed Reading Room was opened in 1857.

With the continued expansion of Empire, printed materials from all over the world made their way into the library, and the collection grew rapidly. The printing of the General Catalogue of Printed Books between 1880 and 1905 made these enlarged collections more accessible to readers. As the Library continued to grow during the twentieth century, new solutions were sought to the problem of storing and preserving its extensive collections in safety. In 1905 the newspapers were moved to a repository in Colindale, North London. The collections of the Patent Office Library, which joined the British Museum Library in 1966, remained at Chancery Lane, while some other parts of the printed book collections were out-housed at sites in London.

Following the establishment of the British Library and the decision to bring together the bulk of the national collection on a single site, construction of the new Library began in 1982. The new building provides a permanent home for some 12 million volumes, and will accommodate many thousands of readers a year in 11 reading areas. Meanwhile, visitors from all over the world can see some of the Library's outstanding treasures on display in the John Ritblat Gallery.

OPPOSITE: *The Humanities Reading Room, opened on 24 November 1997.*
Photograph by Irene Rhoden

CODEX SINAITICUS

The Codex Sinaiticus is a jewel beyond price. It is the Bible written in Greek, around the middle of the fourth century, and is the earliest manuscript of the complete New Testament and the earliest and best witness for some books of the Old Testament. In antiquity and textual importance it is the equal of the Codex Vaticanus in Rome and generally superior to the Codex Alexandrinus (which is also in the British Library). As one of the earliest luxury codices to survive in large part it also forms one of the most important landmarks in the history of the book. The codex is named after the monastery of St Catherine near the foot of Mount Sinai in Egypt. It was discovered there by the German Biblical scholar Constantine Tischendorf in 1859.

Soon after he made his discovery Tischendorf removed the Codex Sinaiticus to St Petersburg and presented it to Tsar Alexander II of Russia. Forty-three leaves that he found on an earlier visit to St Catherine's in 1844 are now in Leipzig University Library. A further few leaves that the monks at St Catherine's discovered in 1975 remain in the monastery.

Codex Sinaiticus, Caesarea (?), mid-4th century AD
British Library Add. MS 43725, ff.244v-245

HARLEY LATIN GOSPELS

The Harley Latin Gospels, written in the sixth century, is one of the earliest known manuscripts of the Gospels in Latin. The text is written in an uncial script – a luxury script using large rounded letterforms.

On the right-hand page is Section 39 of the Gospel of St John (John 5: 11–22). On the left, the scribe has omitted John 5: 4 (also omitted in the oldest Greek manuscripts). Besides the Four Gospels, this manuscript contains probably the earliest complete set of canon tables arranged under a sequence of arches. These were compiled by Eusebius, Bishop of Caesarea, in the first half of the fourth century and formed a vital aid to readers wishing to locate parallel passages within the Gospels.

The Harley Latin Gospels is known to have been in France by the ninth century. It was stolen from the Royal Library in Paris in 1707 by a renegade priest and adventurer, Jean Aymon. Robert Harley, first Earl of Oxford (1661–1724) bought the manuscript from him in Holland in 1713, and it entered the British Museum collection with his library in 1753.

Harley Latin Gospels, Gospel of St John. Italy, sixth century
British Library Harley MS 1775, ff.390v–391

THE FOUR GOSPELS IN CLASSICAL ETHIOPIC

This manuscript contains the text of the Four Gospels, copied in Classical Ethiopic (Ge, ez), in a majestic official script of the Gondarine court (Gondar was the Ethiopic capital from the sixteenth to eighteenth centuries). The patrons of the manuscript were Emperor Yohannes I (reigned 1667–1682) and the Empress Sabla Wangel.

The Gospels is illustrated with many miniatures, including portraits of the evangelists and narrative illustrations placed within the gospel text. This miniature shows Christ healing two blind men (from the Gospel of St Matthew 20, verses 30–34), which is based on woodcut engravings by Dürer, as used by A. Tempesta in the Arabic Gospels published in Rome in 1590–91. This combination of image and text departs from the models of early gospel decoration, in which miniatures were never integrated with the text.

The Four Gospels in Classical Ethiopic, Christ healing two blind men. Mid-seventeenth century
Or. MS 510, f.51

SULTAN BAYBARS' QUR'ĀN

This opening is from volume one of a Qur'ān in seven volumes, copied by the calligrapher Muḥammad ibn al-Waḥīd, and illuminated by Muḥammad ibn Mubādir and Aydughdī ibn ʿAbd Allāh al-Badrī, in Cairo, 704 AH (AD 1304), for the Mamluk Rukn al-Dīn Baybars, at that time High Chamberlain, and afterwards the Sultan Baybars II. This appears to be the only surviving example of the work of this famous calligrapher.

The piece shown here is the first chapter of the Qur'ān, Sūrat al-Fātiḥah, written in the cursive hand known as thuluth. Each of the seven volumes of this Qur'ān is copied in gold thuluth and has a magnificent frontispiece which is illuminated in Mamluk style, characterised by the extensive use of geometrical patterns and ornamental Eastern Kufic script. Qur'āns copied entirely in thuluth are relatively rare. In this copy, the vowels are marked in red, and other spelling symbols, such as sukūn, in blue.

Sultan Baybars' Qur'ān. Calligraphy by Muḥammad ibn al-Waḥīd;
illumination by Muḥammad ibn Mubādir and Aydughdī ibn ʿAbd Allāh al-Badrī, Cairo, 704 AH (AD 1304)
British Library Add. MS 22406, ff.2v–3

GANDHARAN BUDDHIST SCROLLS

These scroll fragments, from an extraordinary trove of birch bark writings from ancient Gandhara, may represent the oldest surviving Buddhist texts (and also the oldest South Asian manuscripts) ever discovered.

Gandhara was a great kingdom straddling present-day Pakistan and Afghanistan, and a vibrant crossroads of Indian, Iranian and Central Asian cultures. At the peak of its influence, from about 100 BC to AD 200, it was perhaps the world's most important centre of Buddhism, and was almost certainly the gateway through which Buddhism was transmitted from India to China and elsewhere, to become one of the world's great religions.

Archaeological evidence for Gandhara's Buddhist culture abounds, but until recently there has been little documentary evidence of its literary or religious canon. The British Library acquired this collection of 13 scrolls, written in Kharosthi script, in 1994, which together represent a substantial proportion of the long-lost Gandharan Buddhist canon. Texts so far identified range from technical and philosophical teachings to popular didactic verse, such as the 'Rhinoceros Horn Sutra' and the 'Song of Lake Anavatapta' represented above.

Gandharan Buddhist scroll fragment. Gandhara, first century AD
British Library Or. 14915.3:I.3

THE GLORIFICATION OF THE GREAT GODDESS

This is a beautiful palm-leaf manuscript of the Devimahatmya, a Sanskrit hymn extolling the Goddess as the Supreme Principle of the Universe. It was copied in Nepal in Newari script in 1549 and illuminated with thirty-two miniatures and painted covers in the reign of Jayapranamalla of Bhaktapur (1523–?1550), for the use of the king.

Hinduism is widely thought of as a religion with a multiplicity of gods and goddesses, but the vast majority of Hindus worship only one of these (normally either Vishnu or Siva) as the Supreme Principle of the Universe, while duly acknowledging a selection of the others for personal worship. Some worship the Goddess (Devi, under various names) as the Supreme Principle, and this Glorification of the Goddess, the most important text in her worship, acknowledges her as encompassing all the other divinities. The upper folio shows the donor and his family worshipping the Goddess in the act of killing Mahishasura the buffalo-headed demon. The lower folio depicts Vishnu asleep on the cosmic ocean with Brahma seated on a lotus emerging from his navel; the newly-manifested Goddess raises the sleeping god to kill the demons menacing Brahma.

Devimahatmya, The Glorification of the Goddess. Unknown artist, Bhaktapur, Nepal, 1549
British Library Or. MS 14325, ff.1v–2

THE LINDISFARNE GOSPELS

The Lindisfarne Gospels is one of Britain's greatest artistic treasures, an outstanding surviving example of Insular Anglo-Saxon and Celtic book painting of the late seventh century. Written and illuminated in honour of God and St Cuthbert about AD 698 probably by the monk Eadfrith, afterwards Bishop of Lindisfarne from AD 698 to 721, it is famous for the superb quality and intricate design of its decorated pages.

A single artist-scribe was responsible for both script and decoration throughout the Lindisfarne Gospels. The volume is painted in a large and subtle range of pigments from animal, vegetable and mineral sources, some of which, notably lapis lazuli, would have been imported to seventh-century Northumbria from Asia. Each of the four gospels opens with a miniature of the appropriate Evangelist, a decorative 'carpet' page based on the form of a cross, and an elaborate initial page.

The Lindisfarne Gospels is of particular significance, not only because of the quality and ingenuity if its decorations, but because of the special interest of its complementary Latin and Old English texts, and the fact that it can be dated and localised with quite extraordinary precision, if its colophon is taken at face value. The colophon was added to the book around 970 by Aldred of Chester-le-Street. This stated that the book was dedicated to God and St Cuthbert, and it is likely that it was in fact completed to honour the elevation of St Cuthbert's relics to the altar. Aldred also added a literal interlinear Anglo-Saxon translation at the same time as the colophon, which is the earliest extant version of the gospels in any form of English language.

The manuscript's carpet and major initial pages (*see* page 4), display the extraordinary richness of Eadfrith's decorative vocabulary, elements of which are drawn from other media, notably jewellery and enamel work, such as that of the early seventh-century Sutton Hoo ship burial.

The Lindisfarne Gospels, portrait of St Mark and his symbol, the lion
Lindisfarne, *c.*AD 698
British Library Cotton MS Nero D iv, f.93v

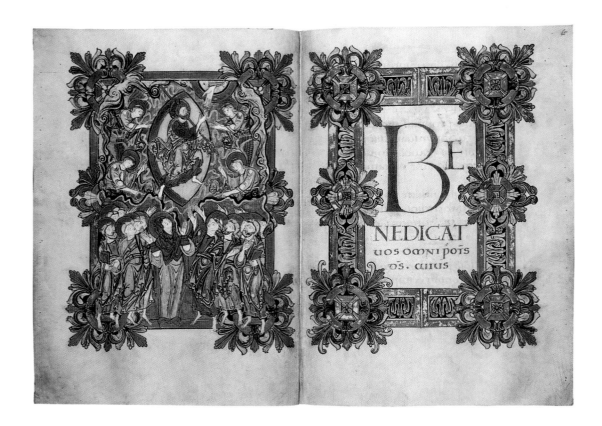

BENEDICTIONAL OF ST ÆTHELWOLD

This manuscript, which was made for the personal use of Æthelwold, Bishop of Winchester from 963 to 984, one of the leaders of the late tenth-century monastic revival in England, is an outstanding masterpiece of later Anglo-Saxon book painting and a major example of the influential so-called 'Winchester style'.

The Benedictional of St Æthelwold contains special prayers for use by the Bishop when pronouncing a blessing over his congregation at mass. It was written out for Æthelwold by a Winchester monk named Godeman, who was apparently his chaplain. Each of the principal festivals of the church year and a number of the most important saints, including Winchester's special patron, St Swithun, are represented among its twenty-eight surviving miniatures. Aethelwold was a major patron of the arts and is himself reputed to have been a skilled worker in precious metals.

Benedictional of St Æthelwold, the Ascension. Winchester, *c.*970–980
Add. MS 49598, ff.64v–65

GOSPELS OF TSAR IVAN ALEXANDER

The Gospels of Tsar Ivan Alexander is the major treasure of a cultural and spiritual Renaissance in fourteenth-century Bulgaria, and a masterpiece of East European manuscript art. The Gospels' creation was not only the supreme achievement of Bulgarian medieval culture; it also marked its final flourishing, 500 years after the introduction of Christianity and the Cyrillic script into Bulgaria, and shortly before the country's collapse under the invasion of the Ottoman Turks.

The work of a single scribe named Simeon, the manuscript was written and illuminated in 1355 to 1356 for Tsar Ivan Alexander. At its front is an imposing double-page portrait of the Tsar Ivan Alexander, together with his second wife, Theodora, and his two sons, son-in-law and three daughters. The volume contains 366 miniatures illustrating the life of Christ.

After the Tsar's death, the Bulgarian Empire disintegrated and its capital, Turnovo, fell to the Turks in 1393. The manuscript was apparently taken into Romania and later reached the monastery of Saint Paul on Mount Athos in Greece. It was discovered there in 1837 by the English traveller Robert Curzon, who contrived to acquire it as a souvenir of his visit.

Gospels of Tsar Ivan Alexander, portrait of the Royal Family. Turnovo, 1355–1356
British Library Add. MS 39627, ff.2v–3

THE BEDFORD HOURS

The Bedford Hours is a superb example of late medieval manuscript art, written and illuminated in the early fifteenth century for John, Duke of Bedford, younger brother of King Henry V, and his wife Anne of Burgundy. The principal artist of the leading Parisian workshop in which it was produced takes his name, the 'Bedford Master', from his English patron.

Expertly planned and executed, the Bedford Hours is celebrated for the enormous range of its pictorial scheme, its brilliantly coloured miniatures and over a thousand exquisite marginal details. This illustration of the Legend of the Fleurs de Lys is narrative rather than devotional. Accompanied by thirty lines of French verse, it tells the story of how the Fleurs de Lys, the royal arms of France, was given by God's angel to the hermit of Joyenval, who in turn entrusts it to Clovis's wife, Clothilda. Clothilda then presents it to her husband, who has been newly converted into a Christian knight. This legend was popular with the dynasties of Burgundy, for Clothilda was a Burgundian princess, and the traditional narrative is therefore used to emphasise the Bedfords' support for any contemporary claim on the French crown. The miniature thus combines elements of legend with Christian and contemporary political references.

The Bedford Hours, the Legend of the Fleurs de Lys
The Bedford Master, Paris, early fifteenth century
British Library Add. MS 18850, f.288v

Comment nuſ ſeigꝰ par ſon ange enuoya les trops fleurs de lis Oꝛ en vn eſcu diſant au roy clouis·

THE DUKE OF SUSSEX'S GERMAN PENTATEUCH

The Pentateuch is part of the Torah, one of the three main sections of the Hebrew Bible, and also the most sacred. It comprises the first five books of the Old Testament.

The Duke of Sussex's German Pentateuch was written and illuminated by a scribe-artist known as Ḥayyim, working in Southern Germany around 1300. The manuscript takes its name from its last owner, the Duke of Sussex (1773–1843), before it became part of the British Museum collection in 1844. Each of the five Old Testament books is preceded by an illuminated opening word set in a full-page miniature. Shown here is the beginning of the Book of Numbers, which describes the arrangement of the twelve tribes of Israel into four camps, each with its own banner. The opening illuminated word is 'Va-yedaber', 'and he spoke', a reference to the Lord speaking to Moses, as found in the first verse of Numbers. The four soldiers in booths hold standards bearing devices traditionally associated with the leading tribes: Judah (a lion), Joseph (a bull), Dan (a serpent), and Reuben (an eagle).

Duke of Sussex's German Pentateuch
Opening of the Book of Numbers. Ḥayyim, southern Germany, *c*.1300
British Library Add. MS 15282, ff.179v–180

THE GOLDEN HAGGADAH

The Haggadah, a type of prayerbook, is the order of service for the celebration of Passover-eve in the home. Traditionally the most richly decorated of all Jewish prayerbooks, Haggadah means literally 'narration' and tells the story of the divine deliverance of the children of Israel from Egyptian bondage.

Written and illuminated in Northern Spain, probably Barcelona, the Golden Haggadah begins with a series of full-page miniatures, executed by two artists, and showing the influence of the Northern French Gothic style of illumination. This opening shows, from the right-hand page, at the top, the destruction of Sodom (Genesis 19); top left the binding of Isaac (Genesis 22); bottom right Isaac feeling Jacob, with Rebecca and Esau (Genesis 27); bottom left Jacob's dream (Genesis 28). On the left-hand page, top right, Jacob and his family cross the river Jabbok (Genesis 32); top left is Joseph's dream (Genesis 37); bottom right shows Joseph relating his dreams to Jacob, with his brothers looking on (Genesis 37), and in the bottom left is Joseph seeking his brothers and their flock and meeting a man – in Jewish tradition the angel Gabriel – who redirects him (Genesis 37).

Golden Haggadah, Biblical scenes. Anonymous artist, northern Spain, probably Barcelona, *c.*AD1320
British Library Add. MS 27210, ff.4v–5

THE MEMOIRS OF BABUR

The Emperor Babur, founder of the Mughal dynasty, was an outstanding military leader and ruler. He was also a highly cultivated and observant man who wrote good poetry and took a keen interest in the history and natural history of India and of his Central Asian homeland. These qualities are reflected in Babur's memoirs, which he began at the age of twelve, in 1494, and continued until his death in 1530.

The Emperor Akbar, Babur's grandson, had these memoirs translated from the original Chaghatay Turkish into Persian, so that posterity could better understand this remarkable man. Four major illustrated copies from the Akbar period are known; this one, produced around 1590, is the largest in scale and includes 141 paintings by at least 54 different artists.

This opening shows on the right the almond harvest at Kand-i Badam, painted by Bhavani, and on the left nine dervishes struggling to protect themselves from a whirlwind in the wasteland called Ha Darvish, painted by Thirpal.

Akbar's copy of *Babur-nama* (Memoirs of Babur): paintings by Bhavani and Thirpal, *c.*AD 1590
British Library Or. MS 3714, ff.6v–7

THE STORY OF THE MONK PHRA MALAI

The Buddhist story of the monk Phra Malai was widely illustrated in Thailand from the late eighteenth century until the early twentieth century. These folding-book manuscripts were produced by well-to-do laymen to offer to temples for use by the monks in their preaching. The presentation of a fine manuscript brought merit to the sponsor and his or her family.

The story tells how Phra Malai journeys to heaven and hell and returns to earth to report what awaits us after we die. Illustrations such as these richly appareled angels hovering in the air are a popular convention in Thai Buddhist imagery and nearly always occur in Phra Malai manuscript illustration as part of the heavenly scenes. The angels' rich clothing, with gold highlights, represents contemporary court dress. The text is in the Thai language but in Cambodian script, which was usual for writing on Buddhist subjects in old Thailand. An inscription added in English records that the manuscript was bought from a Malay or Siamese sailor at Singapore by the Master of a British trading ship and was presented to the British Museum in 1844.

Phra Malai, hovering angels. Anonymous artist, central Thailand, c.1800–1830
British Library Add. MS 15347, f.38

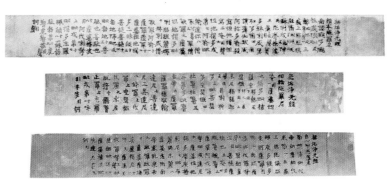

THE MILLION CHARMS OF EMPRESS SHŌTOKU

After the suppression of the Emi rebellion in 764, the Japanese Empress Shōtoku ordered that a million copies of dhārāni (charms or mantras, the recitation of which was meritorious) be printed in thanksgiving. The copies were distributed, each in a miniature wooden pagoda, among the ten leading Buddhist temples in western Japan over a period of six years.

A monumental landmark in the history of printing, these Hyakumantō dhārāni, or 'One Million Pagoda Charms' are the oldest extant examples of printed text in Japan and, until challenged by more recent discoveries in Korea and China, were regarded as the world's earliest surviving printed specimens of proven date. The method of printing continues to be debated but was either from woodblocks or metal plates.

The four texts, selected and transliterated into Chinese script from Sanskrit, are Konpon, Sōrin, Jishinin and Rokudo. Each was printed in two versions: 'standard' and 'variant'. The British Library is one of only two libraries which possesses the complete set of eight texts. The main body of the pagoda was made of Japanese cypress, and the ringed lid of cherrywood.

The Million Charms of Empress Shōtoku. Nara, Japan, 764–770
British Library Or. 78.a.11; Or.81.c.31B (pagoda)

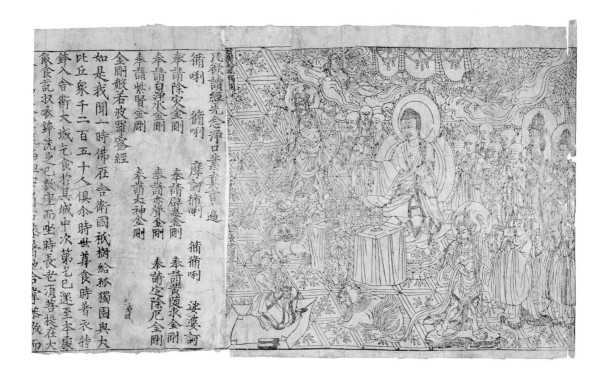

DIAMOND SUTRA

The Diamond Sutra, a Buddhist text produced in China in AD 868, is the world's earliest dated printed book. Printing began in the Far East much earlier than anywhere else in the world. The earliest surviving example of a text printed from blocks, specifically prepared for this purpose, dates from no later than AD 751. The quality of the Diamond Sutra's illustration makes it clear that the blockcutter had a considerable period of experience and skill behind him.

The Diamond Sutra scroll was found in 1907 by the archaeologist Sir Marc Aurel Stein in a walled-up cave at the Caves of the Thousand Buddhas, near Dunhuang, in north-west China. It was one of a small number of printed items among many thousands of manuscripts, comprising a library which must have been sealed up in about AD 1030. A colophon, at the inner end of the scroll, reads: 'Reverently [caused to be] made for universal free distribution by Wang Jie on behalf of his two parents on the 15th of the 4th moon of the 9th year of Xiantong [i.e. 11th May AD 868]'.

Diamond Sutra, frontispiece: Buddha preaches to his disciple Subhuti. China, 11 May AD 868
British Library Or. 8210, p.2

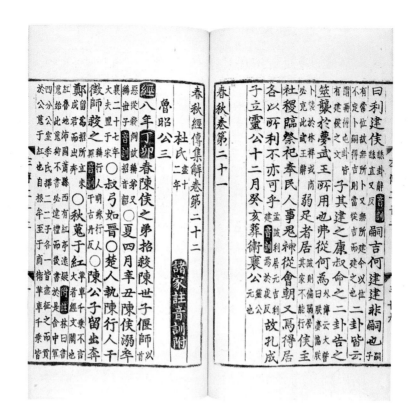

COLLECTED COMMENTARIES ON THE SPRING AND AUTUMN ANNALS

Anonymous Korean metalworkers of the fourteenth century were the world's first printers of moveable type, antedating Gutenberg's famous bible by over seven decades. The survival of a Buddhist text dating from 1377, printed at a provincial temple in south Korea, suggests that Korean artisans had mastered the basic techniques of casting and setting metal type long before the patronage of King Sejong (reigned 1418–1450) resulted in handsome large editions such as the pages shown here.

At the court of King Sejong, cast bronze types were used to print works that ministers and scholars needed for their political and ethical reform programme. Since copies of Chinese texts could be imported from China only with difficulty, court officials persevered in improving type design and setting methods until high-quality type like the *kabin* face shown here was achieved. *Kabin* type displays the influence of the Chinese calligrapher Zhao Mengfu (1254–1322) whose elegant writing style inspired many imitators among calligraphers and printers during the fifteenth century.

'Collected commentaries on the Spring and Autumn Annals'. Ch'unch'u kyŏngjon chiphae, Seoul, 1434
British Library 16015. c. 3

THE GUTENBERG BIBLE

The most famous printed Bible in the world, Gutenberg's 42-line Bible is the earliest full-scale work printed in Europe using moveable type. Printed in Mainz in 1455 by Johann Gutenberg and his associates, Johann Fust and Peter Schoeffer, only forty-eight copies are known to have survived, of which twelve are printed on vellum and thirty-six on paper. Twenty are complete, two of them at the British Library. Many, including the British Library's lavish paper copy, married the new technology of printing with the old, and contain hand-painted decoration so as to imitate the appearance of an illuminated manuscript. The result was a work of exceedingly high quality which set standards for book production which in many ways are still unsurpassed today.

The opening shown is the end of Jerome's *Prologus* and the beginning of Genesis. The illustrations depict scenes from the natural world: birds and flowers, suggesting echoes of Eden. The text is very legible, and is made clearer by the use of highlighted first letters for new sentences.

The Gutenberg (42-line) Bible, Jerome's *Prologus* and the opening of Genesis
Johann Gutenberg, Johann Fust and Peter Schoeffer, Mainz, 1455
British Library C.9.d.3, ff.4v-5

THE SFORZIADA

Giovanni Simonetta's 'Life of Francesco Sforza' (known as the 'Sforziada') is another superb example of early printing decorated with the illuminated borders and ornaments of the manuscript tradition. Francesco Sforza (1401–1466) had claimed the duchy of Milan after the death of his father-in-law and came to power in 1450. His eldest son, Galeazzo Maria Sforza, succeeded him but was assassinated in 1476, leaving only his son, the seven-year-old Gian Galeazzo Sforza (1464–1494). Gian Galeazzo's uncle, Lodovico il Moro (1451–1508), essentially usurped power from the boy, and it was he who ordered the biography of his father Francesco to be written and printed in Latin in 1482. Eight years later it was translated and printed in Italian, further reinforcing Lodovico's reputation as a dutiful son and cultured patron.

Four illuminated copies of the Sforziada survive, richly decorated by the Milanese painter Giovan Pietro Birago. In the British Library's copy, the portrait of Francesco Sforza on the frontispiece is carefully identified with inscriptions, 'PATER PATRIÆ' ('Father of the Country') and 'DUX MIL IIII' ('4th Duke of Milan'). A profile portrait of Lodovico also appears in the roundel opposite. The fusion of printed text and hand-painted decoration testifies to the evolutionary transition from manuscript to print.

The Sforziada, frontispiece to Giovanni Simonetta's 'Life of Francesco Sforza'
(an Italian translation from the Latin)
Illuminated by Giovan Pietro Birago, Milan, 1490
British Library G.7251

LIBRO PRIMO DELLA HISTORIA DELLE COSE FACTE DALLO INVICTISSIMO DVCA FRANCESCO SFORZA SCRIPTA IN LATINO DA GIOVANNI SIMONETTA ET TRADOCTA IN LINGVA FIORENTINA DA CHRISTOPHORO LANDINO FIORENTINO.

FRAN. SFOR. VIC DVX — MLIIII — PATER PATRIAE

NE TEMPI CHE LA REGINA GIOVANNA seconda figliuola di Carlo Re regnaua:perche era succeduta nel regno Neapolitano a Latislao Re suo fratello:elquale parti di uita sanza figliuoli:Alphonso Re daragona con grande armata mouendo di Catalogna uenne in Sicilia : Isola di suo Imperio. La cui uenuta excito gli huomini del Neapolitano regno a uarii fauori:& a diuersi consigli:& non con piccoli mouimenti di quel regno:Impero che Giouana Regina per molti & uarii suoi impudichi amori era caduta in soma infamia. Et desperandosi che lei femina potessi adempiere lofficio del Re:& administrare tanto regno:fece a se marito Iacopo di Nerbona Conte di Marcia:elquale per nobilita di sangue:& belleza di corpo:ne meno per uirtu era tra Principi di Francia excellente. Ma accorgendosi in breue che quello desideraua piu essere Re: che marito:& quella non molto stimaua:mosso da feminile leuita lo rifiuto:& priuo dogni administratioe. Questo fu cagione chel suo regno:elquale per sua natura e prono alle dissensioni & discordie:arrogendouisi e no honesti costumi della Regina : ritorno nelle antiche factioni & partialita:& comincio ogni giorno piu a fluctuare & uacillare. Erano alcuni a quali no dispiaceua la signoria della dona:perche benche il nome fussi in lei:loro nientedimeno comidauono. Altri desiderauano:che Lodouico tertio Duca dangio: figliuolo di Lodouico elquale era nomato Re di Puglia: & di uiolante nata della Reale stirpe daragona:fussi adoptato dalla Regina. Costui poco auati pe conforti di Martino tertio somo Pontefice:& di Sforza Attendolo excellentissimo Duca in militare disciplina : & padre di Francesco sforza de cui egregii facti habbiamo a scriuere era uenuto a liti di Campagna:Et cogiuntosi Sforza:hauea mosso guerra alla Regina. Ma quegli che repugnauano a Lodouicho:metteuano ogni industria: che Alphonso fussi adoptato in figliuolo della Reina:accio che in Napoli fussi tal Re:che con le sue forze & di mare & di terra potessi resistere alla possa de Franciosi . Adunque in cosi uehemete contentione de baroni:& piu huomini del regno:Alphonso chiamato dalla Reina in herede & compagno del regno:diuene no solo illustre: ma anchora horribile : Et el nome Catelano elquale insino a quegli tempi no era molto noto & celebre se non a popoli maritimi:ma inuiso & odioso: comincio a crescere : & farsi chiaro. Ma & da Lodouico & da Sforza tanto ogni giorno piu erono oppressi:el Re & la Regina:che diffidadosi nelle proprie forze:conduxono Braccio Perugino : elquale era el secondo Capitano di militia in Italia in quegli tepi co molte honoreuoli coditioni: & maxime

HORTUS EYSTETTENSIS

In the early seventeenth century the Prince-Bishop of Eichstätt, Germany, created a splendid garden, the first to contain all the shrubs and flowering plants known at the time, including the latest imports from the Orient and America. When the garden was complete he commissioned a monumental picture book of the plants – the *Hortus Eystettensis* ('Garden of Eichstätt'), published in 1613 by the botanist-apothecary Basilius Besler, who had helped to develop the garden.

   Besler's book contained 367 plates printed from elaborately prepared copper engravings. Even in black-and-white *Hortus Eystettensis* was and is the greatest botanical picture book ever created, but a few copies were printed on special paper and individually hand-coloured. This copy, coloured by George Mack, was owned by George III before 1780 and is part of the King's Library.

Hortus Eystettensis, Tulips. Basilius Besler, 1613
British Library 10.Tab.29

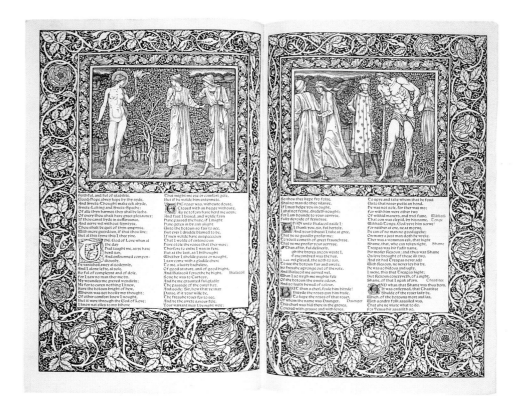

THE KELMSCOTT CHAUCER

The Kelmscott Press was established in Hammersmith, London, in 1891. Founded by artist, writer and social reformer William Morris and Sir Edward Burne-Jones, it was dedicated to the revival of traditional high-quality craftsmanship. This book, the Kelmscott Chaucer, was the jewel in the crown of the press.

Dismayed by the shoddy quality of goods that were being produced in a newly mechanised England, William Morris, with Sir Edward Burne-Jones, founded a furniture and interior design company in 1861. Their furnishings, textiles and stained glass were highly sought after, but it was their impact on book illustration and typography that was to prove most enduring, with the establishment of the Kelmscott Press in 1891.

The Kelmscott Chaucer was produced using Morris's third custom-made typeface (Chaucer) and was illustrated by Burne-Jones. The edition was five years in the planning, and took two years to print; it embodies Morris's and Burne-Jones's dedication to literature, art and craftsmanship.

The Works of Geoffrey Chaucer. Illustrations by Edward Burne-Jones,
engraved on wood by W.H. Hooper, The Kelmscott Press, Hammersmith, 1896
British Library C.43.h.19

BEDE'S 'HISTORY OF
THE ENGLISH CHURCH AND PEOPLE'

Bede's *Historia Ecclesiastica Gentis Anglorum* ('History of the English Church and People')
tells the story of the conversion of the English people to Christianity and is the chief source
of information about English history from the arrival of St Augustine in Kent in 597 until
731. Bede (died 735) spent all his adult life as a monk at Jarrow in Northumbria. He was the
first great English historical writer, and this, his most famous work, shows how Christianity,
at a time when England was still divided into a number of kingdoms, played a vital role
in creating a sense of national identity.

   This manuscript was produced in southern England, in the early ninth century, within
a century of Bede's death. The beginning of Book IV, which describes the events of the year
664 (in which the famous 'Synod of Whitby' occurred), is shown, with the words 'In anno'
(in the year) decorated. Book IV of Bede's work describes the achievements of Theodore of
Tarsus, Archbishop of Canterbury from 668–90, one of the most influential of the early
Archbishops of Canterbury.

Bede's 'History of the English Church and People', opening of Book IV
Southern England, early ninth century
British Library Cotton MS Tiberius C.ii, ff.93v–94

THE ANGLO-SAXON CHRONICLE

The Anglo-Saxon Chronicle is the earliest known history of England written in the English language. It was probably first compiled at the behest of King Alfred (849–899), and distributed to monasteries throughout the country, where each copy was kept up-to-date by a member of the monastic community.

The Chronicle is the oldest history of any European country in a vernacular language. In most versions, the entries cease soon after the Norman Conquest in 1066, but one version continued until as late as 1154. The court origins of the Chronicle mean that its early entries are essentially an official history of the West Saxon royal dynasty (although some Mercian material is drawn upon), but from the late tenth century the entries made in the various versions kept in different monasteries became increasingly independent.

Only seven manuscripts of the Chronicle have survived, of which four are in the British Library. This manuscript formerly belonged to Abingdon Abbey. It was written in about 1046 and contains additions to 1066. The pages shown here contain entries for the years 835 to 854 and describe the first major Viking attacks on England.

Anglo-Saxon Chronicle (C-text), entries for 835–854. Abingdon, mid eleventh century
British Library Cotton MS Tiberius B.i, ff.128v–129

MAGNA CARTA

Magna Carta is one of the most famous of all documents, widely regarded as the corner-stone of liberty in the English-speaking world. It does not, however, contain any sweeping statements of principle; instead its text consists of a series of detailed concessions on legal procedure and feudal rights wrung from an unwilling King John (reigned 1199–1216) by his noble opponents in 1215.

Magna Carta has long been considered the chief constitutional defence against arbitrary and unjust rule in England. It was effectively a treaty of peace between King John and a group of leading noblemen who had rebelled against him for reasons the charter itself makes clear: his financial and military demands to aid his foreign wars were oppressive; taxation was arbitrary and extortionate; the King imposed arbitrary punishments; and feudal rights were ruthlessly exploited for financial gain.

In the course of a meeting in June 1215 between the King and the nobles at Runnymede, near Windsor, a document was presented summarising the nobles' demands. John's Great Seal was fixed to this document to signify his assent to it. The document sealed at Runny-mede is probably that known as the Articles of the Barons, which is also in the British Library. The royal chancery then turned the list of demands into a formal grant in the name of the King. The text of this grant was disseminated in the form of royal letters patent, which were sent to bishops, sheriffs and others throughout the land. Only four of these letters, the 'originals' of Magna Carta, survive. Two are in the British Library; the others are held by Lincoln and Salisbury Cathedrals.

Magna Carta was promptly overturned by the Pope, to whom John had given the over-lordship of England. Civil war was renewed, and John died while still fighting the rebels. The original destination of the document shown here is unknown. It was given to Sir Robert Cotton by the barrister Humphrey Wyems on 1 January 1629, and according to one account had been found in a London tailor's shop.

Royal letter promulgating the text of Magna Carta
England, 1215
British Library Cotton MS Augustus II.106

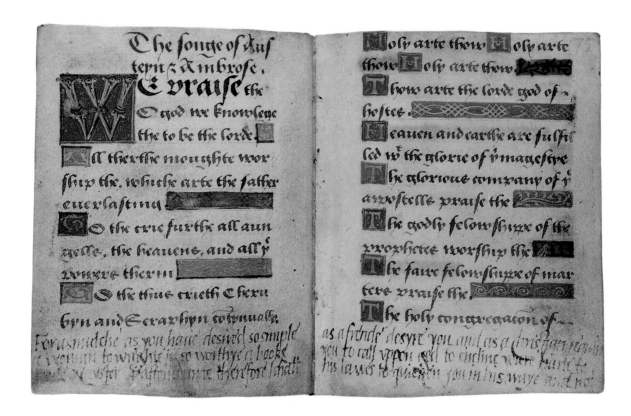

LADY JANE GREY'S PRAYERBOOK

This tiny prayer book is probably that used by Lady Jane Grey on the scaffold at her execution in 1554. After the death of Edward VI on 6 July 1553, his cousin, the 15-year-old Lady Jane Grey, was persuaded by her father-in-law, the Duke of Northumberland, to accept the English throne in order to prevent the accession of the Catholic Princess Mary. After a reign of only nine days, Jane was overthrown in favour of Mary and confined to the Tower of London. On 12 February 1554 she was beheaded.

In the moments before her execution, Jane is said to have given to Sir John Bridges, the lieutenant of the tower, the prayerbook which she had read during her final journey; this is apparently that book. In the margins, she had written various farewell messages including the words, addressed to John Bridges, at the bottom of the pages shown here: 'Forasmutche as you have desired so simple a woman to wrighte in so worthye a booke (good) mayster lieutenaunte therefore I shall as a frende desyre you and as a christian require you to call uppon god to encline youre harte to his lawes to quicken you in his waye and not to take the worde of trewthe utterlye oute of youre mouthe.'

Lady Jane Grey's Prayer Book
British Library Harley MS 2342, ff.74v–75

THE EXECUTION OF MARY QUEEN OF SCOTS

This contemporary drawing from the papers of Robert Beale (1541–1601), the clerk of the privy council, shows Mary Queen of Scots at three stages in her execution. Mary, a Catholic with a a claim to the English throne, was a natural focus for discontent and plots under Elizabeth I. After nearly twenty years in England she was brought to trial in 1586 for complicity in the Babington conspiracy. Despite Elizabeth's indecision, Mary was executed on 8 February 1587 in the hall of Fotheringay Castle, Leicestershire. Beale carried the death warrant to Fotheringay and read it aloud as a preliminary to the execution. The drawing shows Mary entering the hall attended by her women, on the scaffold, and lying on the block with the executioner's axe ready to strike. It does not show her dog which, according to the Dean of Peterborough (figure number six in the foreground) had crept under her skirts and could only be removed after the execution by force.

The Execution of Mary Queen of Scots, 1587
British Library Add. MS 48027, f.650

LETTERS PATENT OF THE EAST INDIA COMPANY

The East India Company was the foundation stone of British colonial expansion in Asia. It was established by royal charter in 1600 at the request of a number of merchants who had agreed to contribute substantial sums of money to finance voyages to the East Indies, present-day Indonesia. Their hopes of obtaining a large share of the valuable spice trade were thwarted by competition with the Dutch and they turned their attention towards India, where during the seventeenth century, a number of factories, or trading posts, were established along the coast. By the late seventeenth century, the East India Company's success provoked increasing resentment among those excluded by its monopoly, and there was considerable political pressure to open up the trade to the east. These letters patent of 1693 would therefore have been of immense importance to the Company, as they confirm its privileges, as well as regulating its activities. The richness of the decoration may well be an indication of the significance attached to them.

Letters patent of the East India Company, 11 November 1693
British Library IOR A/1/48

NELSON MEMORANDUM

In this memorandum, Horatio, Viscount Nelson (1758–1805) explains to his captains his plans for engaging the allied French and Spanish fleet, twelve days before the Battle of Trafalgar. The memorandum, which is an unsigned autograph draft, dated 'Victory', off Cadiz, 9 October 1805, contains Nelson's fullest exposition of his conception of naval tactics and formed the basis of his tactics for the forthcoming battle.

The draft plan of attack – which he called the 'Nelson touch' – was sent to Nelson's second-in-command, Admiral Collingwood. The essence of the plan, now regarded as a masterpiece of naval strategy, is indicated at the bottom of the right-hand page. The fleet was to be drawn up 'in two lines of sixteen ships each with an advanced squadron' of eight of the fastest sailing ships. The intention was, as Nelson states on the left-hand page, 'to overpower [the enemy line] from two or three ships ahead of their Commander-in-Chief supposed to be in the Centre to the Rear of their Fleet'.

Memorandum by Horatio, Viscount Nelson, off Cadiz, 1805
British Library Add. MS 37953

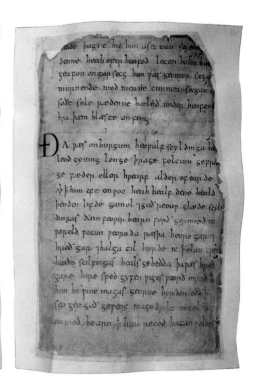

BEOWULF

This is the only surviving medieval manuscript of 'Beowulf', the most important poem in Old English and the first great English literary masterpiece. The poem tells of the feats of the Geatish (Scandinavian) hero Beowulf. In his youth, Beowulf kills Grendel, a monster who had been terrorising the hall of the Danish king Hrothgar, and then slays Grendel's mother, who comes to avenge her son. Later, after fifty years as King of the Geats, Beowulf engages in combat a dragon who has been attacking his people. Both Beowulf and the dragon are mortally wounded.

This manuscript dates from the first quarter of the eleventh century. The exact date at which the poem was composed is a matter of controversy. The most common view is that it was composed in the eighth century, but it has recently been argued by some scholars that the poem is more recent, even perhaps contemporary with the manuscript. Nothing is known about the author of the poem. The text forms part of a volume containing other material in Old English acquired by the Elizabethan collector Sir Robert Cotton, which was damaged in a fire at Ashburnham House in Westminster in 1731. The leaves were mounted in paper frames to protect the brittle damaged vellum in 1845.

'Beowulf'. Anonymous, place of production unknown, first quarter of the eleventh century
British Library Cotton MS Vitellius A XV, ff.133v–134

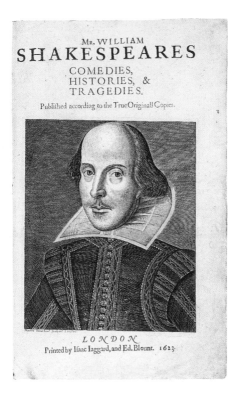

THE SHAKESPEARE FIRST FOLIO

The First Folio, published in 1623, seven years after William Shakespeare's death, was the first collected edition of his plays. It was edited or overseen by his devoted friends and fellow actors, John Heminge and Henry Condell.

Of the thirty-six plays in the Folio, half had already been published as quartos, though of these, four had appeared as 'bad' quartos only. The Folio, therefore, gives the texts of eighteen hitherto unpublished plays. It was printed from sources that represent the plays as performed in the theatre. *Hamlet*, for instance, is two hundred lines shorter than the second quarto text, perhaps because of the cuts made in performance. Behind the First Folio text of *Hamlet* lies a manuscript other than that from which the second quarto was printed, possibly the prompt-book, or a transcript of it, released by the company of actors for publication. The printer understandably preferred to set up type from printed 'copy' rather than manuscript, and the text of *Hamlet* and several other plays in the First Folio may have been set from 'good' quartos which had been collated with this manuscript and amended accordingly.

The Shakespeare First Folio. Title-page incorporating a portrait of Shakespeare
engraved by Martin Droeshout, printed by Isaac Jaggard and Edward Blount, London, 1623
British Library G.11631

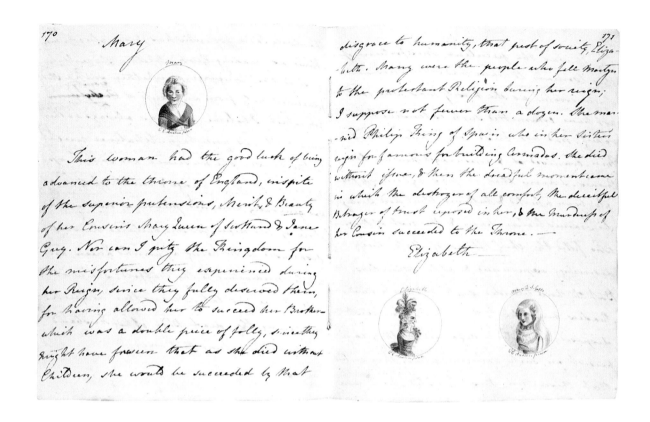

JANE AUSTEN (1775–1817)
'THE HISTORY OF ENGLAND'

'The History of England from the reign of Henry the 4th to the death of Charles the 1st. By a partial, prejudiced and ignorant Historian.' It was with these words that the sixteen-year-old Jane Austen began her study of the English monarchy, a gleeful parody of Oliver Goldsmith's *History of England* published in 1771.

'The History of England' is one of the most precocious and engaging works of juvenilia ever produced by a leading literary figure. Written in 1791, the manuscript is illustrated with delightful medallion portraits of monarchs painted by Jane's sister Cassandra.

From the age of twelve, Jane Austen spent more of her spare time in literary composition than in serious study. She preserved twenty-six items of juvenilia, dating from around 1787 to early 1793, and later copied them into three notebooks entitled Volume the First, Volume the Second and Volume the Third. The 'History of England' appears in Volume the Second, acquired by the British Library in 1977.

Jane Austen's autograph manuscript of 'The History of England', with medallion portraits
(of Queen Elizabeth and Mary Queen of Scots) by her sister Cassandra, 1791
British Library Add. MS 59874, ff.85v–86

On uttering these words, I looked up; he seemed to me a tall gentleman, but then I was very little; his features were large, and they and all the lines of his frame were equally harsh and prim.

"Well, Jane Eyre, and are you a good child?"

Impossible to reply to this in the affirmative; my little world held a contrary opinion. I was silent; Mrs Reed answered for me by an expressive shake of the head — adding soon:

"Perhaps the less said on that subject the better, Mr Brocklehurst."

"Sorry indeed to hear it — she and I must have some talk." And bending from the perpendicular, he installed his person in the arm-chair opposite Mrs Reed's.

"Come here," he said.

I stepped across the rug; he placed me square and straight before him. What a face he had — now that it was almost on a level with mine! What a great nose and what a mouth, and what large prominent teeth!

"No sight so sad as that of a naughty child," he began, "especially a naughty little girl. Do you know where the wicked go after death?"

"They go to hell," was my ready and orthodox answer.

"And what is hell? Can you tell me that?"

CHARLOTTE BRONTË (1816–1855), 'JANE EYRE'

Charlotte Brontë was born in 1816, the fourth of the Brontë children and the eldest of the three sisters who gained fame through writing. Following her unhappy early education at Cowden Bridge school near Kirkby Lonsdale, where her two elder sisters contracted consumption from which they subsequently died, Charlotte was taught at home; she later attended Roe Head School, to which she returned in 1835, at the age of nineteen, to take up a post as a teacher. Charlotte disliked teaching, and following a further period as a student and teacher in Brussels, she returned to the idea that the sisters might earn an income from their writing, in which they were all prolific. Their first publication, a volume of poems which they funded themselves, sold only two copies, but Charlotte was undaunted, and when she submitted the manuscript of her novel *Jane Eyre* to the London publisher Smith, Elder and Co., it was accepted almost immediately and published, in 1847, to critical acclaim. This manuscript is Charlotte's autograph fair copy of the work; the folio shows her description of the tyrannical Mr Brocklehurst, head of Lowton Charity School.

Charlotte Brontë's autograph fair copy of 'Jane Eyre', 1847
British Library Add. MS 43474, f.46

LEWIS CARROLL (1832–1898)
'ALICE'S ADVENTURES UNDER GROUND'

'Alice's Adventures Under Ground' was Lewis Carroll's original version of the work later published as *Alice's Adventures in Wonderland* (1865). The tale was first told by Charles Lutwidge Dodgson, 'Lewis Carroll', on 4 July 1862, to the three young daughters of Henry Liddell, Dean of Christ Church, Oxford, on a river boat trip. The children, especially Alice, adored the story and begged Carroll to write it down. It took him until February 1863 to write out the whole text, taking great pains to write in neat 'manuscript print', designed for the young Alice to read. Once the text was complete, Carroll began to add the illustrations which give a charming impression of his own vision of Wonderland and its inhabitants. The final 90-page manuscript was completed in September 1864, bound in green morocco and given to Alice on 26 November with the inscription 'A Christmas Gift to a Dear Child, in Memory of a Summer Day'.

Urged by friends to publish the work, Carroll expanded the text and removed many private Liddell family jokes and references. John Tenniel was commissioned to provide the illustrations, several of which were based on Carroll's original sketches in the manuscript.

Now one of the British Library's most famous literary manuscripts, 'Alice's Adventures Under Ground' was presented to the British Museum Library in 1948 by a group of Americans, led by the Librarian of Congress, in recognition of the part played by Britain in the Second World War.

Charles Lutwidge Dodgson's autograph manuscript of 'Alice's Adventures Under Ground', 1862–64
Alice drinks from an unlabelled bottle
British Library Add. MS 46700, f.19v

than she expected: before she had drunk half the bottle, she found her head pressing against the ceiling, and she stooped to save her neck from being broken, and hastily put down the bottle, saying to herself "that's quite enough— I hope I sha'n't grow any more— I wish I hadn't drunk so much!"

Alas! it was too late: she went on growing and growing, and very soon had to kneel down: in another minute there was not room even for this, and she tried the effect of lying down, with one elbow against the door, and the other arm curled round her head. Still she went on growing, and as a last resource she put one arm out of the window, and one foot up the chimney, and said to herself "now I can do no more — what will become of me?"

Dulce et Decorum est.

Bent double, like old beggars under sacks,
Knock-kneed, coughing like hags, we cursed through sludge,
Till on the haunting flares we turned our backs
And towards our distant rest began the trudge.
Some marched asleep. Many had lost their boots
But limped on, blood-shod. All went lame; all blind;
Drunk with fatigue; deaf even to the hoots
Of gas shells dropping softly behind.

Then somewhere near in front: Whew...fup, fup, fup,
Gas-shells? Or duds? We loosened masks in case, —
And listened.... Nothing. Far rumouring of Krupp.
Then poison hit us in the face.
Gas! GAS! Quick, boys! — An ecstasy of fumbling,
Fitting the clumsy helmets just in time;
But someone still was yelling out and stumbling,
And floundring like a man in fire or lime ...
Dim, through the misty panes and thick green light,
As under a green sea, I saw him drowning.

In all my dreams, before my helpless sight,
He plunges at me, guttering, choking, drowning.

WILFRED OWEN (1893–1918)
'DULCE ET DECORUM EST'

Most of the poems for which Wilfred Owen is remembered were those he wrote as a soldier in the trenches in an extraordinary burst of creativity between the summer of 1917 and his death in the autumn of the following year. Owen enlisted in 1915 and was sent to France. In 1917 he contracted trench fever, and met fellow poet Siegfried Sassoon while convalescing in Edinburgh. On his recovery, Owen returned to the front line and was killed a week before the end of the war was declared.

One of Owen's most haunting works, this clear and legible autograph draft for 'Dulce et Decorum est' was part of a collection which he was compiling at the time of his death, intended to convey the sheer horror of life at the Front to an ill-informed and largely complacent audience in England. After his death his poems were edited for publication by Siegfried Sassoon, and first appeared in 1920.

Wilfred Owen's autograph draft of 'Dulce et Decorum est', c.1917
British Library Add. MS 43720, f.21

THE OLD HALL MANUSCRIPT

The Old Hall Manuscript contains the oldest surviving collection of English part music. This choir book is made up mostly of settings of the Ordinary of the Mass, together with some antiphons and motets. The majority of the music has not survived elsewhere and the book is of incomparable value as a record of the vital link between the music of the Middle Ages and of the Renaissance in England in the early fifteenth century.

The collection was compiled by a single scribe in about 1410 to 1415, with additions c.1415–1420 by at least seven further hands. It is the earliest English source to present a repertory of works by named composers. The complexity and precision of the notation employed indicates a high degree of sophistication in the writer and the intended users of the book, as well as the composers. The manuscript identifies numerous English composers, including one 'Roy Henry', who is most likely to have been Henry IV himself. A piece attributed to 'Roy Henry' is shown here: a 'Gloria' for three voices. The manuscript takes its name from a previous owner, St Edmund's College, Old Hall Green, in Ware, Hertfordshire.

The Old Hall Manuscript, compiled and written probably for the Chapel Royal in the reign of Henry IV (1399–1413), with additions c.1410–1420
British Library Add. MS 57950, ff.121v–122

GEORG FRIDRICH HANDEL (1685–1759)
'MESSIAH'

The 'Messiah' is probably Handel's most famous composition. Written in 1741, and first performed in 1742, it established him as a truly popular composer at a time when, it was rumoured, he was on the point of leaving England because of the lack of success of his works in the theatre. The text for the oratorio was prepared by Handel's friend and literary collaborator Charles Jennens, and in the summer of 1741 Handel began work on it. By 28 August he had drafted part I, by 6 September part II, and part III is dated 12 September; the completion of the instrumentation took a further two days.

'Messiah' was given its first performance in the New Musick Hall, Fishamble Street, Dublin, on 13 April 1742. It was an immediate success, though the first London performance was received less favourably. It was not until 1750, when Handel gave a benefit performance of the work at Thomas Coram's Foundling Hospital, that its lasting popularity was established.

Handel's composition score is the source from which the many different versions of 'Messiah' derive. From it, copies were made for performance, initially by Handel's principal copyist J.C. Smith, with revisions and corrections by the composer himself.

Georg Fridrich Handel (1685–1759), 'Messiah', autograph composition draft,
'Behold the Lamb', opening of Part II, London, 1741
British Library R.M.20.f.2., f.53

WOLFGANG AMADEUS MOZART (1756–1791)
'THEMATIC CATALOGUE'

The *Verzeichnüss aller meiner werke…* or 'Thematic Catalogue' is Mozart's own list of his compositions from the last seven years of his life and provides a unique record of his creative process. No other great master of music kept such a detailed chronological list of this quality.

Although partial catalogues of some of his early works survive, some kept by his father, Mozart may have started this comprehensive catalogue as an attempt to sort out his chaotic way of working. The volume is in surprisingly good condition for a working journal. The unruled left-hand page of each opening bears the titles or descriptions of the compositions, and, in the case of the operas, the names of the singers at the first performance. Each right-hand page is ruled with ten staves grouped in pairs, on which he wrote the first few bars of the music, in short score where necessary. His last entries include the operas *Die Zaubeflöte* and *La Clemenza di Tito*; composition of the first was interrupted by the hurried completion of 'Clemenza', so 'The Magic Flute' has two entries. The final composition recorded is the little 'Masonic Cantata' which Mozart entered on 15 November 1791, three weeks before he died.

Wolfgang Amadeus Mozart (1756–1791)
'Thematic Catalogue' 1784–1791; the last entries for 1791
British Library Zweig MS 63, ff.27v–28

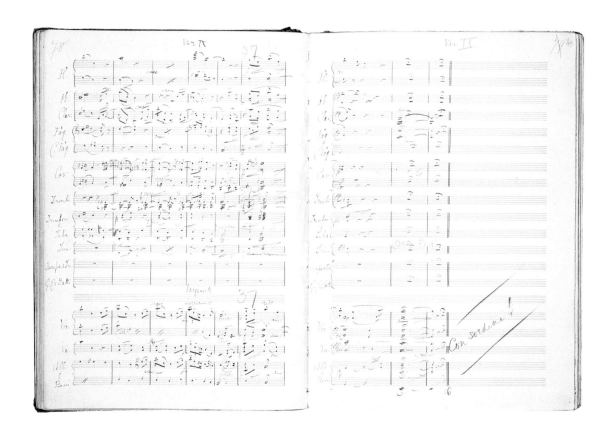

EDWARD ELGAR (1857–1934)
'ENIGMA' VARIATIONS

Elgar's Variations on an Original Theme ('Enigma') portray the characters of a number of the composer's close friends. First performed in London in July 1899, this was one of the first works to bring Elgar to public recognition.

Between the first 'Variation', which represents Elgar's wife, and the finale, a portrait of the composer himself, come the 'Friends pictured within' to whom the work is dedicated. They are identified by nicknames or initials; the best-known of all, Variation XIII, is Nimrod, the mighty hunter, a play on the name of Elgar's publisher and most valued adviser August Jaeger. The Variation was prompted by a discussion between the two men about Beethoven's music; it has become one of the best-known of all English melodies. The 'enigma' of the title remains.

Edward Elgar (1857–1934)
Variations on an Original Theme ('Enigma'), op. 36, 1889 to 1899, autograph, 'Nimrod'
British Library Add. MS 58004, ff.50v–51

I wanna hold your hand.
Oh yea, I'll tell you something
I think you'll understand
when I say that something
I wanna ... ,
Twice
Oh please say to me
you'll let me be your man
and please say to me
you'll let me hold your thing.

And when I touch you
I feel happy inside
It's such a feeling that my love
I can't hide etc ..
Oh you got that something
I think you understand
When I feel that something
I wanna hold your hand.

3/10 See me.

Written in Paul's hand. Composed by
Paul & John in Jane Asher's basement.

JOHN LENNON (1940–1980) AND
PAUL McCARTNEY (1942–   )
'I WANT TO HOLD YOUR HAND'

This manuscript, in Paul McCartney's handwriting, contains the lyrics of the Beatles' fifth single, 'I want to hold your hand', first recorded on 17 October 1963 and released on 29 November 1963. It is one of a collection of manuscripts of Beatles lyrics and letters on loan to the British Library since 1985.

With advance sales of one million copies, 'I want to hold your hand' went straight to Number One in the UK, where it stayed for 21 weeks. It replaced 'She Loves You' at the top, and the Beatles became the first group to have had two consecutive chart-topping singles. In January 1964 it was released in America and became the group's first US hit. John Lennon regarded 'I want to hold your hand' as one of the best songs he wrote with Paul McCartney, commenting that it had a 'beautiful melody'.

Paul McCartney, 'I want to hold your hand', 1963
British Library Loan 86

TREATISES ON ANIMALS AND THEIR USES

This thirteenth-century copy of an Arabic work describing the medicinal properties of parts of animals' bodies was compiled from two treatises: 'The Description of Animals' – an Arabic translation of a work attributed to Aristotle – and 'The Uses of Animals', a work by ʿUbayd Allāh ibn Jibrāʾil ibn Bakhtīshūʿ (died after 1058).

In the Islamic world, interest in animals was reflected in a wide range of secular literature as well as in religious and legal writings. While early Arab philologists were primarily concerned with zoological terminology, later writers devoted themselves to the description and classification of animals.

From the eighth to the eleventh centuries medicine in Baghdad was dominated by four families of Christian doctors who passed down the art of medicine from father to son while serving the Abbasid Caliphs (749–1258). One such family was the Bakhtīshūʿ of whom ʿUbayd Allāh ibn Jibrāʾil was seventh generation. Family members from earlier generations were known either for being directors of the famous hospital at Jundīshāpūr or for translating Galen's works from Greek into Syriac. The opening depicts ʿUbayd Allāh ibn Jibrāʾil ibn Bakhtīshūʿ and the Emir Saʿd al-Dīn. 'The Uses of Animals' is one of a number of medico-scientific works which Ibn Bakhtīshūʿ wrote.

Treatises on Animals and their Uses, Ibn Bakhtīshūʿ and the Emir Saʿd al-Dīn.
Anonymous, thirteenth century AD
British Library Or. MS 2784, ff.101v-102

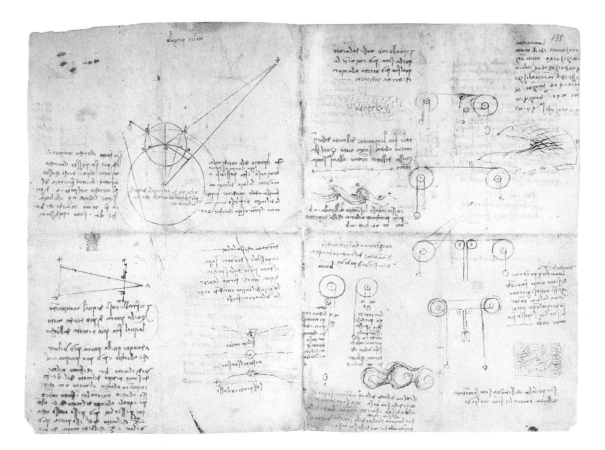

LEONARDO DA VINCI (1452–1519), NOTEBOOK

This autograph manuscript notebook kept by Leonardo da Vinci, known today as the Codex Arundel, was not originally a bound volume, but was put together after his death from loose papers of various types and sizes. The first section was begun at Florence on 22 March 1508, but the remainder comes from different periods in Leonardo's life.

This collection contains short treatises, notes and drawings on a variety of subjects from mechanics to the flight of birds. They are written in Italian, and in Leonardo's characteristic 'mirror-writing', left-handed and moving from right to left. Little is known of the manuscript until its acquisition by Thomas Howard, Earl of Arundel (1586–1646), the greatest English art collector of his day. In 1681 it was presented to the Royal Society by Henry Howard, Arundel's grandson, and transferred to the British Museum in 1831. The sketches on these pages are, on the left, three small diagrammatic drawings of birds in flight; the right-hand page relates mainly to the movement of water.

Leonardo da Vinci (1452–1519), Notebook, *c*.1480–1518
British Library Arundel MS 263, ff.134v-135

MATTHEW PARIS'S MAP OF GREAT BRITAIN

This is the most detailed and artistically finished of the four versions of the map of Great Britain drawn by the artist and historian Matthew Paris, monk of St Albans. They are the earliest maps in existence to show such a level of detail and are outstanding in medieval cartography as genuine attempts to portray the physical appearance of an area rather than reducing it to diagrammatic form.

Matthew Paris was one of the most readable and prolific of medieval chroniclers, producing detailed and well-informed accounts of political events, with vivid descriptions of the main protagonists, discussion of the causes and significance of incidents. He was also an accomplished artist and innovative cartographer. Among many recognisable features on this map are Hadrian's Wall dividing England and Scotland, and the Antonine Wall further north. St Albans features as the first stop north of London, a reminder that much of the information in Matthew Paris's chronicles was gleaned from the conversation of distinguished travellers visiting the Abbey.

Matthew Paris (died 1259), Map of Great Britain, St Albans, *c*.1250
British Library Cotton MS Claudius D.vi, f.12v

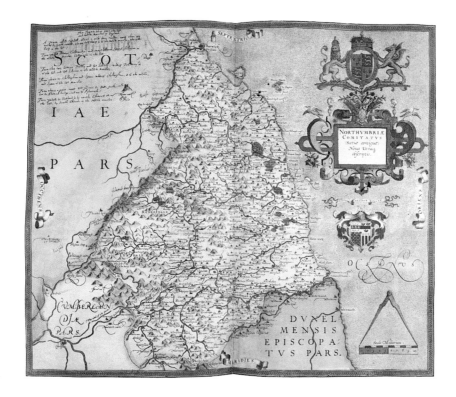

CHRISTOPHER SAXTON'S
MAP OF NORTHUMBERLAND

In the course of the 1570s, Christopher Saxton successfully mapped all the counties of England and Wales, working under the patronage of a leading lawyer, Thomas Seckford. An atlas containing all the maps – the first English county atlas – was published in 1579.

Elizabeth I's ministers, and particularly her Lord Treasurer, Lord Burghley, saw how useful such maps could be for government and administration, and the Crown actively supported Saxton's surveying work throughout the 1570s. As soon as uncorrected proofs of the maps came off the press, they were sent to Burghley, and incorporated into his archives, with his own annotations. This is one of the maps annotated by Burghley, partly in his own hand. His main contribution, going all the way round the edges of the map, was an extensive list of the main landowners whose estates lined the border or marches with Scotland, and the number of horses that they could raise. With this map in front of him, Burghley would have known from exactly where the Queen could call up her troops to defend her lands from Scottish invasion or to discipline an overmighty subject should the need arise.

Christopher Saxton, Northumbriae Comitatus, annotated in the 1580s by Lord Burghley and others; surveyed by Christopher Saxton, engraved by Augustine Ryther (?), probably 1576
British Library Royal MS 18 D. III, CXXI.35

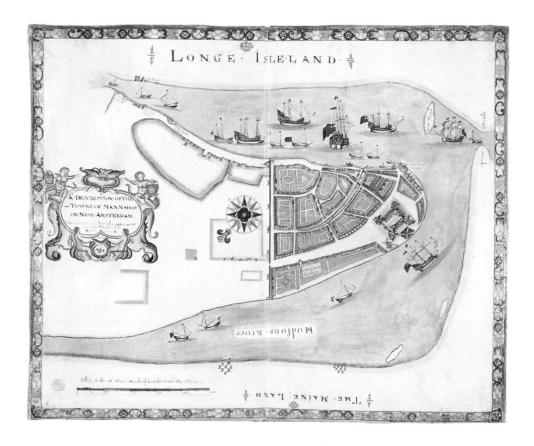

THE DUKE'S PLAN OF NEW YORK, 1664

This anonymous plan, entitled *A description of the towne of Mannados or New Amsterdam as it was in September 1661*, is probably an English copy of a map made for the Dutch authorities in 1661 by Jacques Cortelyou. The Dutch original may have been handed over to the English following their surrender of the town in September 1664.

The map may well have been created by one of several draughtsmen working in the docklands east of the Tower of London who specialised in decorative chartmaking. English ships can be clearly seen in the harbour, emphasising their victory over the Dutch. The town wall, that was to give its name to Wall Street and the Battery (or fortification), the site of which is now covered by Battery Park, can also be identified. The map's name recalls its presentation to the Duke of York, the future James II, at the time when his permission was being sought to rename the town after him. The map formed part of the royal map collection, eventually being incorporated in the geographical collections assembled by George III, and presented to the British Museum, with George III's library, in the course of the 1820s.

The Duke's plan of New York, 1664
British Library K. Top. CXXI.35

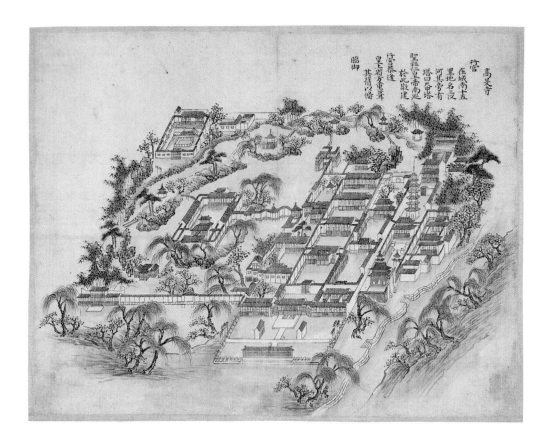

THE JOURNEY OF THE QIANLONG EMPEROR

The Qianlong Emperor (1711–1799) of China made six trips of inspection to the Yangtze area. The places where he stayed were recorded in fine illustrated albums for the imperial archives. One of the paintings in this album was signed by Qian Weicheng (1720–1772). Some of the places where the Emperor stayed were well-known beauty spots, while others were specially-constructed garden-houses, or long-established temples.

This illustration shows a temple with side buildings reached by garden walkways, a pagoda and a fanciful swastika-shaped pavilion (the swastika being the Buddhist emblem of good fortune). The style of the album is unusual for it combines aspects of map-making with landscape painting. Some illustrations are straightforward plans, with the buildings seen as from above; in this one, though the plan of the site and the layout of the buildings are clear, the more painterly depiction of the elements in the garden and surrounding landscape soften the map-like aspect.

The stations of Qianlong's fifth journey, Autumn Sky Temple, possibly by Qian Weicheng,
eighteenth century
British Library Or. MS 12895

BOOKBINDINGS

The Library's outstanding collection of bookbindings includes many masterpieces of major binders or workshops, and important documents of the history of the craft, as well as unique witnesses to the skill of unknown artists and craftspeople. Many royal bindings came to the British Museum in the Old Royal Library, but the collecting of examples of binding as items of historical or artistic interest in their own right properly began with the bequest to the Museum of the collection of Clayton Mordaunt Cracherode (1730-1799), the first English collector of books bound for Jean Grolier, an enterprising patron of the great sixteenth-century bookbinders.

This embroidered binding is believed to be the copy of *De antiquitate Britannicae Ecclesiae* presented to Elizabeth I by its author, Matthew Parker, Archbishop of Canterbury. Queen Elizabeth I (reigned 1558–1603) was given many gold-tooled leather bindings as gifts, but her personal preference seems to have been for velvet bindings. Although the structure of this binding would have been made in a workshop, the decoration would have been sewn by a professional embroiderer.

Matthew Parker, *De antiquitate Britannicae Ecclesiae*, upper cover. London, 1572
British Library c.24.b.8

NEWSPAPERS AND STAMPS

The Library's newspaper collection runs from the first newsletter of 1513 to today's papers, and includes outstanding holdings for the seventeenth and eighteenth centuries, largely collected by George Thomason (died 1666), a London bookseller, and Charles Burney (1757–1817). Now housed at the Newspaper Library in Colindale, North London, the collection is a treasure-house of the topical information which once occupied the daily or weekly attention of millions of British people. It includes many rarities, some of which have become rare through disposal and damage over time, while others were printed in limited numbers at the outset. The circulation of *The Mafeking Mail*, for example, produced during the siege of Mafeking, was restricted, for obvious reasons, by the shortage of raw materials.

Like newspapers, stamps originally issued in large numbers can become rare, or are of special rarity and interest because of mistakes in engraving and printing. The Library's collection of philatelic materials owes its foundation to Thomas Keay Tapling who in 1891 bequeathed his collection, then valued at £50,000, to the British Museum. The present collection, which numbers over six million items, is virtually complete in all issues of adhesive postage stamps from 1840–1889, and is rich in many areas since. This Great Britain 1d red (1858–79, unused) is one of a handful known from printing plate 77, which had been rejected as unsatisfactory, though a few copies from it somehow reached the public.

ABOVE RIGHT: *The Mafeking Mail*, 'Special siege slip… issued daily, shells permitting', 10 February 1900 ('121st day of siege')
ABOVE LEFT: Great Britain 1d red (1858–79, unused)

FURTHER READING

Janet Backhouse, *The Illuminated Page: ten centuries of manuscript painting in the British Library* (London and Toronto, 1997)

Janet Backhouse, *The Lindisfarne Gospels: a masterpiece of book painting* (London and San Francisco, 1995)

Janet Backhouse, *The Bedford Hours* (London, 1993)

Nicolas Barker, *Hortus Eystettensis* (London and New York, 1994)

Nicolas Barker and the curatorial staff, *Treasures of The British Library* (London and New York, 1988; paperback edition London 1996)

Michelle P. Brown, *Anglo-Saxon Manuscripts* (London, 1991)

Michelle P. Brown, *The British Library Guide to Writing and Scripts: History and Techniques* (London and Toronto, 1998)

Michelle P. Brown, *Understanding Illuminated Manuscripts* (London and Malibu, 1994)

Sally Brown, *The Original Alice* (London, 1997)

Yu-Ying Brown, *Japanese Book Illustration* (London, 1988)

Martin Davies, *The Gutenberg Bible* (London and San Francisco, 1996)

Ekaterina Dimitrova, *The Gospels of Tsar Ivan Alexander* (London, 1995)

Mirjam Foot, *Pictorial Bookbindings* (London, 1986)

David Goldstein, *Hebrew Manuscript Painting* (London, 1985)

P. R. Harris, *A History of the British Museum Library* (London, 1998)

Hilton Kelliher and Sally Brown, *English Literary Manuscripts* (London, 1986)

Jerry Losty, *Indian Book Painting* (London, 1986)

Philippa Marks, *The British Library Guide to Bookbinding: History and Techniques* (London and Toronto, 1998)

Bezalel Narkiss, *The Golden Haggadah* (London and San Francisco, 1997)

Elaine Paintin, *The King's Library* (London, 1989)

T.S. Pattie, *Manuscripts of the Bible: Greek Bibles in The British Library* (London 1981; second edition 1996)

Andrew Prescott, *English Historical Documents* (London, 1988)

R. Schoolley-West, *Stamps* (London, 1987)

John Westmancoat, *Newspapers* (London, 1985)

Frances Wood, *Chinese Illustration* (London, 1985)

ACKNOWLEDGEMENTS

The British Library Souvenir Guide was written by Heather Crossley and Anne Young, with curatorial advice from: Janet Backhouse, Colin Baker, Chris Banks, Peter Barber, David Beech, Michelle P. Brown, Sally Brown, Yu-Ying Brown, Penny Brook, Martin Davies, Chris Fletcher, Elizabeth James, Jerry Losty, Philippa Marks, Scot McKendrick, Beth McKillop, Michael O'Keefe, Ann Payne, Andrew Prescott, Arthur Searle, Bart Smith, Ilana Tahan, Muhammad Isa Waley, and Frances Wood.
The British Library is grateful to Sir Paul McCartney for permission to reproduce the manuscript of 'I want to hold your hand'.

© 1998 The British Library Board
First published 1998 by The British Library, 96 Euston Road, London NW1 2DB

Cataloguing in Publication Data: A catalogue record for this title is available from The British Library

ISBN 0 7123 4586 8

Designed by Gillian Greenwood
Colour origination and printing by BAS Printers Ltd, Over Wallop, Stockbridge, Hampshire